The Lovers' Bedside Companion

Romantic Inspiration & Meditations

Gregory J.P. Godek

The history of humankind is the story of our search for love.

The Lovers' Bedside Companion

Romantic Inspiration & Meditations

From Gregory J.P. Godek author of

The following are trademarks of Casablanca Press, Inc. & Gregory J.P. Godek:
"LoveStories," "LoveLetter," "365 Days of Romance," "A Little Romance," "LoveTalks"
"1001 Ways To Be Romantic," "The Lovers' Bedside Companion," "Romance 101,"
"The Portable Romantic," "America's #1 Romantic," "Casablanca Press"
These trademarks denote a series of books and products including newsletters,
calendars, audio cassettes & videotapes.

First printing.
Printed in the good ol' U S of A
10 9 8 7 6 5 4 3 2

Published by
Casablanca Press, Inc., P.O. Box 226, Weymouth, MA 02188 • 617-340-1300

Cover calligraphy by the awesome Maria Thomas at Pendragon Ink • 508-234-6843

Publisher's Cataloging in Publication Data
Godek, Gregory J.P., 1955- / The Lovers' Bedside Companion

ISBN 1-883518-01-6

Dedication

To Linda—We miss you.

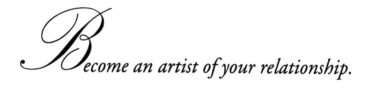

Become an artist of your relationship.

Other books by Gregory J.P. Godek

1001 Ways To Be Romantic

1001 *More* Ways To Be Romantic

Romance 101

The Portable Romantic

Casablanca Press, Inc.

Boston ✦ Sydney

Bookstore distribution: Login Publishers Consortium
800-626-4330

Giftstore distribution: Sourcebooks
800-727-8866

Intimate communication takes place heart-to-heart.

Introduction

This book will be most effective if it is read when you are in a quiet, meditative mood. Thus, as the title suggests, your bedside would be an ideal place to keep *The Lovers' Bedside Companion.*

This book was compiled at the request of readers who asked for "A handbook of romantic inspiration . . . the distilled wisdom hidden amid the flood of romantic tips that comprises Greg's lectures . . . a book that is *slow-paced,* if you know what I mean."

Yes, we know what you mean, and here it is! This collection of quotes and tips is taken from Greg Godek's acclaimed Romance Seminars. Some of these items have appeared in his first three books: *1001 Ways To Be Romantic, 1001 More Ways To Be Romantic,* and *Romance 101.* The focus of *The Lovers' Bedside Companion* is to *inspire* you . . . to make you *think.* We also want to inspire you to *action.* Thus, each quote is accompanied by *practical* suggestions that will help you bring your love *alive.* (A *purely* practical companion to this book— *The Portable Romantic*—is now available. It presents a numbered listing of hundreds of new romantic ideas, tips and resources.)

Thank you for your commitment to bringing more love into *your* life, into your *partner's* life and into this world that so desperately needs it.

Everything else is *easy* compared with love. You can learn the secrets of the atom. You can become an Olympic athlete. You can send a man to the moon.

But there's no instruction book or guru who can teach you a *sure-fire, guaranteed* method for achieving lasting love in your life.

And yet *love* is what it's all about! Welcome to the mystery, the challenge, the journey. *Onward!*

Creating a loving relationship is the most difficult, time-consuming and complicated challenge you will face in your entire life.

Romance resides in the everyday.

Don't wait until Valentine's Day! Those who find romance in the day-to-day activities of their lives know the true secret of happiness.

The "I love you" telephone call from work. The unexpected "Trinket Gift." The afternoon of quiet lovemaking. The evening without TV. The weekend *away* from the kids. The weekend *with* the kids—celebrating your love as a family. The lingering kiss.

Fast or slow?

Gold or silver?

Now or later?

Large or small?

Today or tomorrow?

Red or blue?

Classic or avant-garde?

Conservative or outrageous?

Public or private?

Expensive or not?

Modern or antique?

Here or there?

Give your partner choices.

Love doesn't teach, it shows the way. Love doesn't lecture, it just loves!

Positive reinforcement is the *only* technique that works for motivating another to be more romantic. Nagging creates resentment; guilt generates fear; withholding creates distance.

You can't *teach* love, but you *can* model loving behavior. *You* be the one to start the romantic ball rolling.

Be different!

Go on a picnic. In your living room. At midnight. In the nude.

Fill his car with balloons.

Fill her briefcase with jellybeans.

Re-create her bridal bouquet for your next anniversary.

Rent a costume. Show-up at home as a cowboy.

Greet him at the door with confetti.

Romance is the process . . .
Love is the goal.

A is for ardor, attitude, anniversary, accolades.

B is for boudoir, bed & breakfasts, beaches.

C is for champagne, candlelight, chocolate.

D is for dancing, dinner, diamonds, and dating.

E is for erotic, exotic, emeralds, earrings, Elvis.

F is for flirting, France, fantasies, and flowers.

G is for gifts, get-aways, Godiva, garters, Greece.

H is for hearts, hugs, Hawaii, honeymoons.

I is for intimacy, inns, Italy, islands, ice cream.

J is for jazz, jacuzzis, jewelry, journeys, java.

K is for kissing, kinky, kittens, Koala bears.

L is for lingerie, love, lace, Leo (Buscaglia), laughing.

*True romance is a **voluntary** expression of love, not an **obligatory** gesture performed out of duty or guilt.*

*Romance is a **state of mind.** It's not so much **what** you do as **how** you do it.*

M is for Mozart, m&m's, mistletoe, marriage.

N is for nurturing, negligee, nightcap, novelty.

O is for outrageous, outdoors, opera, orgasm.

P is for passion, Paris, pearls, picnics, poetry.

Q is for quiet, Quebec, quaint, QE2, quirkiness.

R is for roses, Rome, rendezvous, rituals.

S is for singing, sex, silly, sassy, sentimental, sensual.

T is for talking, teasing, toasts, theatre, togetherness.

U is for unexpected, urges, uxorious, union, undress.

V is for violets, Venus, Valentines, Victoria's Secret.

W is for wine, weddings, walking hand-in-hand.

*Romance is a **state of being**.
It's about taking **action**
on your feelings.
It's a recognition that
Love in the abstract
has no real meaning at all.*

Romance is a bridge between the sexes. Our romantic gestures speak clearly and elegantly when we cannot find the right words.

X is for eXcellence, Xmas, Xerography, X-Rated.

Y is for young-at-heart, yachts, yin & yang.

Z is for zany, Zodiac, zeal, zings, Zanzibar.

How did you meet? Do you remember the exact time and place? Was it love at first sight? Or did your love grow over time?

Do you celebrate one another at any time except for your anniversary? Why not celebrate your anniversary every month?

True romantics know that celebrations need not be big, extravagant or expensive!

Romance is the appreciation of two people who are celebrating the lucky coincidence that they found each other.

*Couples who are truly committed to **staying** together attempt to **change** together.*

Change something in your life, in your routine—it can have a great effect on your relationship! Get up an hour earlier every day this week. Take a half-day off work this Friday. Change the way you greet each other.

How can you be committed to your wedding vows *if you don't even* **remember** *your wedding vows?!* Memorize your wedding vows. Or write a *new* set of vows! Have your vows written in calligraphy, frame them, and hang them on your living room wall.

Write a love letter that describes all the reasons you're committed to your lover and to your relationship.

Commitment requires daily renewal. A promise kept, an action made, over and over and over and over and over and over again.

*The goal of **negotiating** is to get as much as you can for yourself. Whereas the goal of **compromising** is to give as much as you get.*

All successful relationships involve compromise. You don't compromise *yourself* or your *values*, you compromise actions and behaviors, attitudes and expectations.

The "Win-Lose" model may work in the outside world, but it wreaks havoc inside intimate relationships.

When one person compromises, he loses. When *two* people compromise, you *both* win.

A great question to ask often is, "What's best for our *relationship*?" Strong relationships support and nurture *both* individuals.

What do you enjoy *doing* together? Do you spend enough *time* together?

How are you *different* when you are with your partner? How does he or she bring out the *best* in you?

How can you nurture your *relationship*—as opposed to just each other?

When a "me" and a "you" decide to become a couple, a new entity called "Us" comes into being.

*You can't control a relationship. It's not like driving a car— it's more like flying a kite. You have **some** say in where it goes, but not a lot!*

Efforts to change or control your partner ultimately suffocate the true uniqueness that attracted you to one another in the first place! Take an honest look at yourself and the control strategies that you may (unconsciously) employ—and work to overcome them. Try letting your partner make all the decisions for a week; switch roles the following week. What insights are generated?

All couples argue and fight—but it's not a *battle*, for crying out loud! Healthy arguments spiral upward toward solutions and intimacy, while harmful arguments spiral downward toward stalemate and bitterness.

Some rules for fighting fair: 1) Stick to the issue, 2) Stay in the present, 3) Say what you feel when you feel it, 4) Focus on changing *behavior*—not each other, 5) Don't accuse.

The "Battle of the Sexes" is a foolish concept. Just think about it . . . If one side won the war, what would we do, take the opposite sex prisoner?!

Romance is the environment in which love flourishes.

What *is* love? I don't mean *philosophically*. I mean *practically*.

What is love to *you*? What behaviors make you feel cared-for and loved? What gives you pleasure? What could your partner do—*specifically*—to make you feel more loved?

Love isn't love until it's acted upon.

A relationship is an act of creativity. You either re-create your relationship each and every day, or you're stuck with something old, inadequate, boring, and ultimately, unsatisfying.

How could you celebrate your anniversary more creatively? Write a love poem. Make a 10-foot-tall anniversary card. Buy a vintage bottle of wine from the year you got married!

To be loving is to be creative. To be creative is to express love.

*He who never asks for help
never gives the gift of
allowing others to share
their love.*

Don't forget that love is about giving *and* taking! Do you have a good balance of giving and taking in your relationship? Give your time. Take your time. Give yourself. Take a walk. Give a backrub. Take it off! Give your love.

Allow your lover to enter into the private recesses of your mind and your heart. Allow the love in.

Speaking our feelings is necessary. But when you reach the point of needing to convey "I love you more than I can say"—that's when a simple kiss can say it all.

Words express passion. Kissing confirms it.

*Practice "Couple Thinking":
View yourself as a member
of a couple first.
Think of "us" and "we"
before "me" and "I."*

Our culture tends to put too much emphasis on rugged individualism, and not enough emphasis on relationship-building and connection-making. Strong couples support strong individuals. "We" and "us" are stronger than "you" or "me" alone.

True intimacy is possible only if you know and understand your partner deeply. In order to do this you must listen—really *listen* to your partner. It helps if you're open-minded, flexible, playful and non-judgmental. Give your partner your *undivided* attention for 30 minutes today.

*True romance is an expression that goes beyond the roses and bubblebaths. It's more subtle than any gift—any **thing**. It's softer than a whisper. It's quieter than words.*

Romantic gestures have no ulterior motive.
Their only purpose is to express love.

Arrive home next Tuesday with a bottle of champagne—just **because**.

Giftwrap a wishbone in a jewelry box. Send it to your partner with a note that says,"I wish you were here."

Rent the romantic movie classic *Casablanca*.

You can touch your partner with your *eyes*. Research shows that eye contact is just as important as physical touch.

You can touch your partner with your *words*. They don't have to be eloquent—just true and heartfelt.

You can touch your partner with your *actions*. It's okay to be a person of few words—*if* your actions speak loudly enough.

To love is to touch . . . with our hands, with our hearts.

*Gifts are symbols.
They represent you—your
feelings, your love—when
you're not physically
there.*

Do you know what the difference between a "gift" and a "present" is?

A *gift* is something that the *receiver* wants. A *present* is something that the *giver* wants the receiver to have.

One is not better than the other, simply different. Gifts say more about the *receiver*: You've listened to her. Presents say more about the *giver*: They express your feelings.

The wedding merely affirms the marriage.

A marriage is a creation of two individuals who turn a relationship into a long-term commitment.

Romance—"love in action"—
is a daily,
changing,
challenging,
exhilarating,
living,
growing
activity.

Romance often *starts* as a "state of mind," but it must move *beyond* mere thoughts and intentions, and be communicated to your lover . . . through words, actions, gifts, gestures, or just a tender look.

Romance is not a one-time thing. It's not something that's "accomplished," and then forgotten. In order to work, it's got to be an ongoing thing—a part of the very fabric of your daily life.

*Romance is a **process**—it's not an **event.***

*Over time, your romantic gifts
should inspire,*

excite,

amuse,

surprise,

console,

connect,

build understanding,

reveal yourself,

and deepen intimacy.

Favorite gift catalogs:

Wireless: 800-669-9999

Rick's Movie Graphics: 800-252-0425

The Nature Company: 800-227-1114

Playboy: 800-423-9494

The Sharper Image: 800-344-4444

Attitudes: 800-525-2468

Seasons: 800-776-9677

Worldwide Games: 800-888-0987

Two threats to romance that are an inherent part of our modern world and American society are Information Overload and Responsibility Overload. Just think of the time you'd free-up if you cut your TV viewing by 50%, and your club/committee responsibilities by 25%!

It's much easier to be romantic when your life is simpler.

GREAT!

*Love is subtle,
and therefore often overlooked.
Love is quiet,
and therefore sometimes lost
amid the noise.
Love is gentle, and therefore
thought to lack strength.
But love powers the universe
and every heart in it.*

Love is empowering. Love is the most powerful force in your life. Loving and giving create abundance. *Giving* is more empowering than *taking*. (How's *that* ✓! for a paradox?!) The more you give of yourself, the more you *have* to give.

Try giving to your lover. Give your time, your attention, your caring, your love . . . Expect nothing in return, and watch miracles happen.

Genuine romance has no ulterior motive. It is about the expression of love, pure and simple. Granted, this is a lofty goal that is only *occasionally* attained, but it's definitely a *worthy* goal. It's certainly fine if *some* romantic gestures impress. But beware of the lover whose romantic gestures never reveal much about himself, and are always extravagant, expensive, showy and glitzy.

Ask yourself: "Does this gift or gesture
1) Build intimacy and trust, or
2) Merely impress?"

*Romance is the expression
of love.
It's the **action** step.
It's bringing love **alive**
in the world.*

Without romance, love becomes merely an empty concept.

What action have you taken recently to express your love to your partner?

Place a rose on the windshield of her car. Hide a love note in his briefcase. Send a Valentine card in August. Create a cassette tape of favorite love songs.

Being in a couple is about *learning* from one another. Don't forget that learning implies growth; it requires time and patience, and it involves making mistakes before "getting it right." And, of course, there's no end to the learning.

What have you learned about your partner in the last week? Sit down and have a conversation this weekend, and don't stop talking until you've both discovered something *new* about each other.

A relationship is a learning experience.

*You can only be **truly known** in an intimate, long-term relationship.*

The paradox is that being "truly known" is a *scary* thing—and *at the same time* a *comforting* thing. We all have conflicting feelings about this process that range from desire to fear. Are you truly known by your partner? Do you truly know your partner?

There's no short-cut to being truly known. It requires open communication over time.

It doesn't matter *where* on the circle you begin. Just so you keep moving through the process.

Romance expresses love.

Love creates intimacy.

Intimacy enhances trust.

Trust builds commitment.

Commitment is the cornerstone of monogamy.

Monogamy flourishes amid romance.

Romance expresses love . . .

The most overlooked factor in successful relationships is maturity.

Only mature people can create happy long-term romances. Why? Because the multitude of skills required to navigate through the long and tumultuous journey of life are acquired only through experience that builds into wisdom.

You can have everything else going for you, but if one or both of you are not mature, you'll either fall into destructive patterns, sink into depression, or drift apart.

Those who expect perfection are *always* disappointed. Those who try to be perfect are *always* failures. If you're expecting your partner to be perfect, you're holding him or her to an impossible standard—one that you *yourself* have never achieved!

Relationships are about trying. And learning. And laughing. And working. And playing. And trying. And doing. And being. And loving.

Ya don't gotta be perfect— ya just gotta keep tryin'!

Relationship problems aren't **always** *deep-seated. Sometimes it's just a "romantic stalemate."*

Strategies for breaking a "Romantic Stalemate," in which neither partner will budge, waiting for the other to take the first step:

Recognize that your relationship is *not* a contest. There's nothing to "win" or "lose."

One of you swallows your pride for one quick minute, "gives-in," and starts the romantic ball rolling. Guaranteed, you'll gain more from this "surrender" than from "holding your ground."

It's the *meaning* that matters, not the *words*. It's the intention that counts, not its specific mode of expression.

Practice listening to your partner. Listen for the meaning behind his actions. Listen for the message behind her words.

Good listening is an active process, not a passive concept.

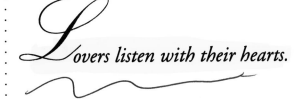

Lovers listen with their hearts.

Romance is never about sacrifice. If your "giving" is reluctant or forced, it's not really romantic.

Romantic gestures enhance *both* the giver and the receiver. Thus, in a way, being romantic is a selfish act! For if you, the giver, don't benefit, there's something wrong in the "Romantic Equation." If you don't derive equal enjoyment from the giving as your partner does from the receiving, then the two of you have unresolved issues to work through.

Throughout our lives we struggle with dependence, independence and interdependence. Dependence is related to immaturity and lack of self-esteem; independence is related to healthy growth—if not taken to extremes; interdependence is the most mature stage of growth.

"Love is generally confused with dependence; but in point of fact, you can love only in proportion to your capacity for independence," said Rollo May.

Mature couples understand and practice interdependence.

43

Return to the classics.

A single red rose.

Dinner at a fine French restaurant.

A fine gold locket with your photo inside.

Casablanca.

A moonlit stroll.

Godiva Chocolates.

A bottle of Dom Perignon.

"Your song."

Write and record a love song for your lover.

Create a "This Is Your Life" videotape.

Pose for an erotic "fantasy photo"!

Create a new mixed drink and name it after your lover.

Write the "Longest Love Letter in History": Write one paragraph per day, every day, for a *year!*

Be creative!

✓

Planning doesn't destroy spontaneity, it creates opportunity.

B_e prepared for spontaneous romantic escapes! Have "His" and "Hers" overnight bags packed at all times. Keep them under your bed or in the car trunk.

B_e prepared for anniversaries, birthdays and holidays ahead of time: Buy gifts and warehouse them in a "Gift Closet."

The decision to say "yes"
or "no" is made and
re-made every day. You
always make a choice,
regardless of whether it's
made consciously or
unconsciously. If you let
the decision be unconscious
or automatic, you're
giving-up some of your
power, and you're robbing
yourself of the joy of
re-commitment.

Saying "yes" with feeling
and awareness is an
empowering act. One that
builds intimacy.

*Consciously re-commit yourself
to your relationship every day.*

Some thoughts for women . . .

Ladies, let's stop . . . male bashing . . . assuming that *all* men are Romantic Boneheads . . . feeling superior about your relationship skills (which often *are* superior!) . . . putting-down the Men's Movement . . . being a martyr . . .

And start . . . giving him the benefit of the doubt . . . meeting him halfway . . . appreciating his quirks . . . putting yourself in his shoes . . . sending him flowers.

Guys, let's stop . . . feeling threatened by feminism . . . stereotyping women . . . assuming we know what they think . . . acting superior . . . ignoring our feelings . . .

And start . . . being real . . . getting in touch . . . reviving gallantry . . . giving of yourself . . . making your relationship a top priority . . . listening more.

Some thoughts for men . . .

*A relationship paradox: When two people explore and appreciate their **differences**, it can bring them closer than ever!*

Isn't it curious that when we fall in love we're *fascinated* with our partner's differences . . . and when we fall *out* of love we claim that it's *because* of those differences?!

Where do your opinions about the opposite sex originate? Have your views been updated in the past decade? Many people are surprised to discover that their opinions were locked-in during childhood or adolescence, and haven't been re-evaluated in years!

Are you dealing with your partner from a framework created in the 1940s, 1950s, 1960s? Are you dealing with the real person or with a stereotype?

Take a good hard look at your beliefs about the opposite sex.

Passive people never live passionate lives.

I've never been able to figure-out why so many people settle for less than exciting, passionate lives. You *deserve* an exciting life, and a passionate relationship.

Getting what you deserve requires confidence, positive self-esteem, and a willingness to take responsibility for your relationship and your life. (Nobody said it would be *easy*—but man, the rewards are *incredible!*)

The price of intimacy is high. And the risk is great. The price is *yourself*. And the risk is abandonment, loss or humiliation. These are major, and understandable barriers.

What about the reward and the promise of intimacy? People who experience intimacy with their partners are *known*. They've got a safe harbor, and this helps them deal with the world much more effectively. They have more inner peace than most people.

Lovers have an inner resource that takes them beyond the limits of what one person alone can achieve.

good words :)

Say the words that your lover wants to hear.

Of course there's always "I love you." But what *other* words are especially meaningful to your lover? The lyrics to a favorite song? The words from a special poem? Your wedding vows?

What words would your lover love to hear you say?

"I believe in you."

"I want you."

"You're the best."

"I cherish you."

"I adore you."

Bouquets of flowers are fine . . . but creative romantics have reported:

Homemade bouquets of chocolate chip cookies.

Homemade bouquets of $10 bills.

Homemade bouquets of tea bags.

Homemade bouquets of autumn leaves.

Take a classic romantic idea and give it a creative twist!

*Definition of marriage vows:
"A declaration of
interdependence."*

When you're in a committed relationship, it's not a choice between *commitment* and *freedom*. You don't give up your freedom when you become a couple. If you *do*, you're either in an immature relationship or a controlling one.

Mature relationships are a dynamic interaction of interdependence and independence. True commitment is a voluntary, freely chosen thing. You must be independent in order to make that choice.

A gentle touch; a simple gesture; a kind word; a wink of an eye; a simple gift; a big surprise; a little surprise; a dinner out; an evening alone; a hot bubble bath; a moonlit stroll; a walk on the beach; a day in the park; a night at the opera; a secret message; a special song.

The expressions are myriad, the meaning is one: "I love you."

*Intimacy is not required 24 hours a day. But it **is** required some time during every 24-hour period.*

Don't let a day go by without connecting in a meaningful way with your partner. Hundreds of "little" gestures over time are more important than one "grand gesture" that attempts to make up for lost time.

Some small but significant building blocks of intimacy: Private jokes, pet names, silly messages, "your song," love letters, love notes, bear hugs, gentle kisses.

Romance can be an occasional thing or an all-encompassing thing. Beginners are allowed to be haphazard about their expression of love. But the true masters know the benefits of *consistency of effort*. They express their love with ease, without thinking about it.

With practice, romance becomes as natural and all-pervasive as breathing. And while breathing keeps your body alive, romance keeps your *soul* alive.

*Being romantic occasionally is one thing, but **living a romantic life** requires consistency of effort.*

Because romantic moments are charged with emotion they create positive memories that last a lifetime.

The past is home to fond memories. The past is a vast and rich reservoir of experiences and learnings for us to draw from. Tapping into your past together can be a powerful romantic resource. If you honor your past, you can use it to help you appreciate the present and build a more fulfilling future.

Have you created any romantic memories recently?

You can compromise without compromising *yourself*.

You can change without losing your uniqueness.

You can grow without growing apart.

You can give without losing *anything*.

You can open-up without being judged.

You can disagree without arguing.

You can feel without losing control.

*You can be romantic
without changing who you are.*

Carpe diem.

Seize the day!

Make a list of 10 things you *know* your partner would *love*. Don't put this off until later—*do it right now!*

Okay, now pick *two* items to implement during the next week. And then you get to pick one item per week for the next eight weeks.

And *then* what? Why, you write a new list, of course!

Without romance, sex is just seduction.

Without romance, sex runs the risk of becoming manipulation or exploitation.

Without romance, sex can turn into an empty habit or dull duty.

With romance, sex becomes connected to love.

With romance, sex is about *giving*, and not merely *taking*.

Romance focuses sexuality toward a loving purpose: The growth of intimacy.

Become an artist of your relationship.

Creativity arises out of dynamic tension. Tension between freedom and discipline, chaos and order, old and new, passion and routine, knowledge and faith. Relationships contain all of the tensions and challenges listed here. The difference between romantics and everybody else is that romantics embrace these tensions as creative challenges, while others see them as problems or threats.

How many years would you like to live?

What's your favorite month?

If you were an animal, what kind would you be?

Ideally, how often would you like to have sex?

What three adjectives best describe you?

Where in the world have you always wanted to visit?

Never stop asking your partner questions.

Intimate communication takes place heart-to-heart.

Communication between lovers must occur on *parallel channels* in order for it to be successful. Everyday communication takes place *head-to-head*, but *intimate* communication takes place *heart-to-heart*. Things will always get messed-up when you try to talk heart-to-head.

You'll lose every time if you use romantic gestures to barter for favors or forgiveness.

Romance is the expression of your love for that special person. It's not a bargaining chip. When you use it as one, you cheapen the gesture, devalue your relationship, and up the ante for the next round of bartering.

Romance isn't barter!
If it's not freely given,
or free of hidden intent, it's
not really romance.

*Advice for singles only: "Think Like a Married Person, Strategy #1"— **Intimacy.***

Although you can't *force* intimacy, you *can* make it a goal. When you think about it, many goals of single folks are *short-term* at best, and downright *shallow* at worst: "Scoring," relieving loneliness, finding a great dance partner.

If, instead, *intimacy* is your goal (*emotional* intimacy, that is), you'll share more of yourself sooner, you'll communicate honestly, and you'll listen to the other more attentively.

When is the last time you actually *flirted* with your own spouse? There's no law against it, you know.

We all enjoy being pursued, we all enjoy a little extra special attention. You could learn something from your single friends.

Advice for marrieds only: "Think Like a Single Person, Strategy #1"— Flirting.

Advice for singles only: "Think Like a Married Person, Strategy #2"— **Long-term thinking.**

The single brain is consumed with *short-term* goals: Do I have a date this Friday night?—What will I wear?—Will he kiss me tonight?—Will she sleep with me on the second/third/fourth date?

Chill-out, singles! Adopting a long-term mindset will relieve a lot of your stress, help you be more "yourself," and give you a better perspective on things.

The typical mindset of a married person is *long-term*. The *positive* side is that this can mean security, commitment and comfort; the *negative* side is that it can also mean boredom, laziness and non-activity.

One way to combat this negative side is to adopt the mindset of a single person: It's a mindset of **instant gratification**. Horny?—Make love *now*. Thinking of her?—Call her *now*. Appreciate him?—Hug him *now*.

Advice for marrieds only: "Think Like a Single Person, Strategy #2"— **Instant gratification.**

*Advice for singles only:
"Think Like a Married
Person, Strategy #3"—*
Communicating.

Have you ever noticed that single people often do a lot of talking without really communicating much? The singles scene is often characterized by a lot of posturing, boasting and clever bantering. Those who get beyond these things have the opportunity to truly connect and become known, and thus begin the journey toward true intimacy.

When is the last time you *seduced* your spouse? How often do you bother to "set the mood," play the music, dress the part, say the right words, do the little things?

Being seduced in the context of a loving relationship is like having your cake and eating it, too!

Advice for marrieds only: "Think Like a Single Person, Strategy #3"— **Seduction.**

*Advice for singles only: "Think Like a Married Person, Strategy #4"— **Becoming known.***

What is dating *about*, for you? For many, it's about *impressing* their date. But for the savvy few, it's about *becoming known*. Married folks don't often tie themselves into knots trying to impress their partners, trying to be the person they think the other wants. Singles who take off their protective masks are often rewarded with meaningful connections with their dates.

One of the biggest dangers of married life is complacency. The security and comfort can lead to laziness. We no longer take *risks*, we no longer stretch ourselves. It's no wonder the passion withers away.

Singles take much bigger emotional risks on a regular basis than marrieds do. The rewards are passion, joy, and wonderment. A little risk-taking within a marriage has the potential to energize your relationship in incredible ways!

Advice for marrieds only: "Think Like a Single Person, Strategy #4"— Risk-taking.

You can't learn intimacy from a book!

Not *this* book, not *any* book! Intimacy must be experienced, lived-with, experimented-with. The best we authors and lecturers can do is point the way. [Actually, that's not true. The *best* we can do is to practice what we preach.]

Please, *please* remember that *you* are in charge. What's important is how *you* feel and how *you* react and how all of this stuff can be integrated into the unique individual that *you* are.

Love is an idea, a concept, a feeling. Love finds its expression in romance.

The language of love takes many forms. Some are spoken. Some are acted upon. Some are purchased. Some are created. Some are written. Some are felt.

Romance is the language of love.

Write it!

Write "I love you" on the bathroom mirror with a piece of soap.

Write it in huge letters on the driveway with chalk.

Write a love letter.

Write a lovesong.

Write 10 love notes on Post-It Notes, and stick them on the refrigerator, in his car, on her pillow, in his briefcase, in his cereal box, on the TV screen . . .

Say "I love you" in Japanese: "Ai shite imasu."

In Russian: "Ya lyubluy tyebya."

In Eskimo: "Nagligivaget."

Recite your wedding vows to one another on your anniversary.

Make "I love you" the first words out of your mouth every morning, and the last words you speak every night.

Say it!

Do it!

Write a steamy love letter.

Learn to say "I love you" in sign language.

Visit Loveland, Colorado.

Give him a one-hour massage, complete with scented oils.

Have your wedding vows rendered in calligraphy and framed.

Take dance lessons together.

The CD "Unforgettable," by Natalie Cole.

A bottle of expensive champagne.

$50 worth of greeting cards.

A lingerie gift.

The book *Love*, by Leo Buscaglia.

A dozen candles.

Buy it!

The Golden Rule doesn't always work! Try instead, "The Platinum Rule."

"Do unto others as you would have them do unto you" would lead workaholics to buy their partners briefcases; golfers to buy their lovers putters; and handymen to buy their wives tools!

Try "The Platinum Rule" which states, "Do unto others *as they want to be done unto.*"

Think about it.

Why is it that men, who understand the importance of *practicing* in sports, have such a hard time practicing relationship skills?

Why is it that women, who understand the importance of *patience* in childrearing, have such a hard time being patient with men, as they slowly learn intimacy?

Celebrate your similarities.
Honor your differences.

Let other things speak for you.

You don't have to be eloquent in order to be romantic! You don't have to write great poetry or even mediocre love letters.

Let these people speak for you: William Shakespeare, Billy Joel, Paul McCartney, Charlie Brown, Susan Polis Schutz, Elizabeth Barrett Browning, Kahlil Gibran.

Let these *things* speak for you: Stuffed animals, flowers, greeting cards, songs, comic strips.

Take that *extra step* and create a flower arrangement that has symbolic significance. For example: Send a dozen roses: 11 red roses and one white one. The note: "You're one-of-a-kind!"

Create a multi-part "theme gift": Wrap into one box: A copy of *The Joy of Sex*; a copy of *The Joy of Cooking*; a new set of pots and pans; and some sexy lingerie.

The best gifts function on several levels: Practical, emotional and symbolic.

Romance is "Adult Play."

Look at what adults have done with the concept of *playing*. We've structured it; we've removed the spontaneity; we've scheduled it; we've raised our expectations unreasonably high; we keep score; and we've turned it into a businesslike, competitive exercise.

What a shame!

How could you really *play* with your partner this weekend?

At its best, a relationship is a dynamic, ever-changing process whereby two people share everything from their joys to sorrows. In a healthy relationship, that process involves playing different roles at different times: I'm strong while you're weak; you're confident when I'm insecure.

In a healthy relationship there's a dynamic shifting of roles that takes place continuously. Healthy couples flow into and out of and around each other.

Great relationships change, grow and evolve.

The best relationships are well-balanced.
*Not a **delicate** balance;*
*not a **static** balance—*
*but a **dynamic**,*
ever-changing balance.

Good relationships balance *over time*. This means that at any particular point in time, the relationship may appear to be quite *unbalanced*: One partner may be more nurturing; one may be more needy; one may be providing all the financial support, etc. But if both partners are loving, understanding, giving, dedicated and flexible, then the relationship can handle all kinds of ups and downs, and still be strong, exciting—and, yes, romantic!

Love cannot be used to manipulate. If one person is manipulating another, there is a lack of love.

People do *not* stay in abusive relationships because of love! They stay because they're scared; they believe they don't have options, or they have low self-esteem.

Love heals, it *does* not—*cannot*—hurt.

*Love does not—**cannot**—hurt. It's the **absence** of love that hurts.*

*Time is **not** money!*

You can save money, but you *can't* save time to use later.

You can create *more* money—by working harder or longer, but you *can't* create more time.

So . . . I suggest that you *save the money* (perhaps for a gift or special event)—but *spend the time now*, while you still have it!

When you come right down to it, *time* is all you really have to give to another person. (The money that you use to buy gifts with is really just time that you've traded for cash, right?!)

When you give time with love you create intimacy.

Time is your most precious commodity. You give yourself when you give your time.

If your relationship were a painting, what would it look like?

What *style* of artwork is it? How does your relationship today compare with the rough sketches of your earlier relationships? What color is it? How do the two of you share the work of creating it? How will you know when it's complete? Is it part of a series? Are you happy with the progress you're making?

What are you committed to? Are you committed to your wedding vows—or the terms of your prenuptial agreement? Are you committed to *forever*—or to *convenience*? Are you committed to excellence—or to mediocrity? Are you committed to remaining independent; or are you stuck being dependent; or are you committed to the more difficult (but vastly more rewarding) path of *interdependence*?

*Are you committed to **forever**— or to **convenience**?*

Choose well.

Romance is *not* the answer to all of your relationship problems. The most romantic person in the *world*, if matched with an inappropriate partner, will be *miserable*—or at least very sad and confused. It takes two *well-matched* people to create a successful relationship. (Notice I *didn't* say *perfectly*-matched.)

Don't settle for a relationship that doesn't provide for your core needs: Emotional and spiritual—as well as practical and financial. When you "settle" you diminish the entire quality of your life; you de-value yourself. **No one** should "settle"! We all deserve wonderful, loving, expressive, growing relationships.

Don't settle.

Respect him
> *Give to him*
> *Trust him*
> *Care for him*
> *Share with him*
> *Laugh with him*
> *Love him*
> *Romance him*

Be a good sport. Indulge him (occasionally). Respect him (always). Share your fantasies with him. Surprise him. Walk a mile in his shoes. Ask his parents about his childhood. Arrange a surprise three-day weekend at a romantic bed & breakfast.

Talk from the heart. Listen more than you talk. Propose a toast. Indulge her passions. Act on her fantasies. Memorize her favorite poem, or the lyrics to her favorite love song. Take an afternoon off work, and spend it together.

*K*now her
Love her
Appreciate her
Remember her
Talk to her
Listen to her
Cherish her
Romance her

In what direction is your passion pointing you? Follow it!

Are you in touch with your passions? Can you hear the Voice within? Are you following your Life's Work? Have you heard your Calling? Does your relationship support your deepest needs? Can you give to your partner without feeling diminished?

You can make all kinds of everyday events into "little celebrations"—opportunities to express your love for your partner. A tiny bit of forethought can turn the ordinary into the special.

Eat dinner by candlelight. Tie a ribbon around a cup of bedtime tea. Turn his birth*day* into a birthday *month*! Leave a greeting card on his car seat.

Turn the ordinary into the special.

Revive chivalry.

Kiss her hand with a *flourish!*

Proper etiquette dictates that you lower your head to her hand; you do *not* raise her hand to your lips!

Warning: You just might fall in love all over again.

Note: The Surgeon General has determined that it is possible to succumb to infatuation at any age.

Fact: A passionate, one-minute kiss burns about 26 calories.

Give your lover 15 minutes of **undivided attention** *every day.*

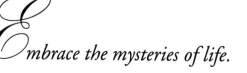

Embrace the mysteries of life.

Experiment with some non-traditional methods of exploring your life, your psyche, your fate, your soul.

Have your handwriting analyzed.

Have your astrological birth charts analyzed.

Have your Tarot Cards read.

Get *every recording ever made* by his favorite musical group.

Get *every book ever written* by her favorite author.

Rent *every movie* starring his favorite actor.

Get *25 pounds* of her favorite candy.

Overdo it!

Great relationships require equal parts of passion, commitment and intimacy.

Passion alone is just a fling.

Commitment alone is a hopeless, aching relationship.

Intimacy alone is too fragile to last long.

Passion and commitment without intimacy is a shallow relationship.

Commitment and intimacy without passion is flat and unexciting.

Passion and intimacy without commitment is short-lived.

Find obscure recordings by her favorite singer.

Get him Season Tickets for his favorite sports team.

Wrap all her gifts in her favorite color.

Get a first edition book signed by his favorite author.

Get her a movie poster from her favorite film.

Avoid generic gifts.

The anticipation is often just as much fun as the event or gift itself.

Always have at least one set of tickets for an upcoming event tacked to your bulletin board. It's always good to have some special event to look forward to.

Celebrate birth *months* instead of just birth*days*.

There is only one place where intimacy can be found: It's in the *now*. You can find hints, advice and great quotes in the *past*. But intimacy isn't simply an *idea*—it's an *experience*. And experiences happen *now*.

Intimacy must be created and re-created. It's not an accomplishment that sits like a trophy on your mantle. It's a feeling, an experience, that is only alive in the moment, in the *now*.

Intimacy isn't simply an idea—it's an experience.

*Money can't buy you love . . . but it **can** buy you a little romance!*

Buy one blue gift and three red ones.

Find two gifts for under $5—three gifts for $20-$25—and one gift for $50-$100.

Get two sentimental gifts— one gag gift—and one practical gift.

January is Nat'l Hobby Month. February is Creative Romance Month. March is Poetry Month. April is Nat'l Humor Month. May is Better Sleep Month. June is Nat'l Rose Month. July is Nat'l Picnic Month. August is Romance Awareness Month. September is Jazz Month. October is Country Music Month. November is Nat'l Stamp Collecting Month. December is Read-A-New-Book Month.

*Celebrate **something** every month.*

Your shared experiences and joint memories weave a tapestry that combines your two lives into one.

Recall with your partner memories that are: funny . . . sexy . . . tender . . . absolutely *hysterical* . . . erotic . . . loving . . . gentle . . . embarrassing . . . profound . . . wild & crazy.

The *good* news is that you're not starting from scratch. The *bad* news is that Life won't stop intruding.

Get up half an hour early; make love with the sunrise.

Eat dinner by candle-light—every night this week.

Spend 30 minutes perusing greeting cards—buy $25 worth.

Hold a "Romantic Idea Brainstorming Party" with some good friends.

*Creating romance is **easy**. It's **re**-creating romance that seems to give people a hard time.*

Places hold special memories for us.

Visit the place where you first met.

Return to the site of your first date . . . your wedding . . . your honeymoon . . . your first apartment.

Your mood, your attitudes, your emotional well-being, your entire mental health are all affected by what you think about. So why in the world do so many of us start our days by poisoning our minds with the news on TV, radio and newspapers? Why not try an alternate routine? —Start your day by talking with your lover in bed for 15 minutes.

Be careful of what you put into your head.

Do you have 20 years of experience—or one year of experience repeated 20 times?

Experience does not necessarily equal wisdom. You must learn from your mistakes in order to acquire wisdom.

If you *like* each other, the details won't get in the way. If you *dislike* each other, the details will be insurmountable.

What attracted you to each other in the first place? How have each of you changed and grown since you first met?

It doesn't matter if you were lovers before you were friends. But you must *develop* a friendship with your lover.

*Do you **like** your lover as much as you **love** him or her?*

*N*obody **said** this was going to be **easy!**

You cannot be known unless you open your heart.

You cannot love without being vulnerable.

You cannot be intimate without taking a risk.

You cannot share feelings in a non-supportive environment.

You cannot enter a relationship demanding a guarantee.

You cannot be controlling and spontaneous at the same time.

Are you a *passive* listener or an *active* listener? The **passive** listener is focused on *himself* ("How does what she's saying affect me?"). The **active** listener is focused on his *partner* ("What is she feeling? Do I really understand what she's saying?").

Be an active listener.

The essence of romance is communication.

Give your lover your undivided attention.

Eliminate the phrase "Yes, but . . ." from your vocabulary.

Don't interrupt your partner.

Practice empathy. Put yourself in your partner's place.

Suspend your judgment.

Listen with patience.

Listen with your heart, not your head.

The speed of Love is *slow*. Very slow. It is linked to your natural self. Average walking speed is 2 miles per hour. Average heart rate is 70 beats per minute.

In contrast, the speed of Life in America in the 1990s is *fast*. Very fast. It is linked to the marvels of technology: Computers processing at 100 million bytes per second; speed limits of 65 miles per hour.

Slow down!

What is the speed of love?

Love is not a mystery to be solved. It is an experience to be savored.

Do you savor meals together, or rush through them? When's the last time you watched a sunset? A sunrise? When's the last time you slept-in late? When's the last time you spent more than one hour making love?

It doesn't matter if you're a truck driver or a school-girl; a man or a woman; a youngster or an oldster; rich or poor; western or eastern—we're all the same. Our emotions, motivations, psyches, wants and needs are all essentially the same. The variations and differences comprise a thin—but important!—layer of uniqueness. We need to honor the uniqueness while acknowledging the Oneness underneath it all.

Deep down we're all the same: We all want to be loved, cared-for and appreciated.

There is no secret when it comes to love. There is only living it.

There are no short-cuts. There are no secret strategies. There are no Ten Commandments.

There is only living it. Trying it. Learning from our mistakes and trying again. Feeling the frustration. Holding the uncertainty. And growing from the experiences. And trying yet again.

Despite civilization's sophistication and technology's innovations, every person must go through the same stages of personal development, discovery and maturation that every human being in history has struggled through. (That's both frustrating and comforting, isn't it?)

Yes, we live in a modern, sophisticated age—but we still feel ancient, primal emotions.

*J*ust because love is a
mysterious, emotional thing
doesn't mean you have to
approach it like a moonstruck
teenager, innocent child or
melodramatic movie star.

There are consistent, logical patterns of action that lead to success. There are beliefs and attitudes that create intimacy. There are choices that build trust. There are strategies that lead to long-term happiness.

Is it *really* a paradox that parents who keep their love for *each other* at the center of their lives are also the most loving and caring parents?

The best way to teach love to children is by example.

Parents who martyr their relationship for the sake of their children are not doing them any favors.

*Sex is easy.
It's love that's **hard.***

Why do humans have such difficulty with the basic concept of sex—while animals take to it so easily? Because we've entangled sex with love. For us, sex is no longer just a physical experience—it is also an emotional experience, and potentially a spiritual experience.

Sex is an incredible melding of our animal nature and our spiritual nature.

Take a little sex, stir-in a generous portion of love, and you get—*lovemaking*.

Some modest suggestions: Make love without using your hands. Make love with your eyes closed. Make love without uttering a word.

Love makes the world go 'round.
Sex makes the ride fun.

he root of our problems—
all of our problems—
is a lack of love.

The power of love is always a giving, expansive, joyful, creative thing. It is *impossible* to twist love into a negative purpose. So don't blame love for your problems. The root of our problems—*all* of our problems—is a lack of love.

It's that simple. And that hard.

You want change? —Change *yourself!* You're the only one you really have any control over.

Actually you *can't* change another person. You can only create a climate that is *safe* for change; that is *supportive* of change; that is *patient* with the time it will take to change.

A marriage license is not a license to change your partner.

*You have the **right** to be appreciated. You also have the **responsibility** for looking out for your own best interests.*

The partner who is unhappy with *any* relationship situation has the responsibility for initiating the conversations that will bring about change. If you don't take some action, you're playing the martyr.

Are you a business executive? Create a "Love Plan" based on a Business Plan. Now implement it!

Are you a gardener? Apply patterns of organic growth to your relationship. Do you have strong roots? Does your relationship need more water (refreshment), sunshine (energy), fresh air (activity)?

Are you a teacher? Write a "Relationship Curriculum."

Look for "patterns of success" in your life. Apply them to your relationship.

Relationships aren't 50/50—they're 100/100.

You are both equally responsible for your relationship. This doesn't mean 50/50—a nice, equally-balanced equation. It means 100/100. You're both 100% responsible for the state of your relationship. (This holds true *regardless* of whether or not you *accept* this responsibility!)

This is why immature people rarely have long-lasting relationships. This is why those who marry young often struggle so much.

Before you can accept responsibility for a relationship, you must accept responsibility for yourself.

Love is more than just a feeling. It is a life-long journey of self-discovery.

And even though maps and guides can help you through the journey, the key thing here is that you have to make your *own* journey. You have to live it. You have to take your own risks. You have to find your own way.

Sit in front of a roaring fireplace.

Get tipsy on champagne.

Climb a mountain.

Walk a beach.

Watch a sunrise.

Escape to a romantic bed & breakfast.

*Love. Don't waste precious time trying to **define** it. Spend your time **experiencing** it!*

Through your intimate relationship, you and your partner experience the beginnings of Oneness.

The search for wholeness permeates our lives. Whether we're conscious of it or not, our motivations, decisions and actions move us toward the achievement of this ultimate goal.

Growth. Fulfillment. Wholeness. Inner Peace. Flow. Centeredness. *Oneness.* Our love relationships are intimately connected to this goal.

Some define a *couple* as "Two, in the process of becoming One."

Do you know his or her . . . favorite color, lucky number, favorite flower, favorite perfume, dream vacation spot, favorite author, favorite book, favorite fairy tale, favorite Bible passage, favorite song, favorite singer, favorite magazine, favorite cookie, favorite ice cream, favorite comedian, favorite movie, favorite sports teams, favorite season, favorite time of day, favorite comic strip, favorite wine?!

How well do you really know your partner?

*Romance is expressing **your** feelings in **your** way.*

Romance is not about "giving-in" to what your partner wants. *Don't* give-in. *Don't* do what she expects. *Don't* do what society expects. *Don't* try to live-up to some fairy tale of what the perfect partner should be.

Instead—be yourself, express yourself, do it *your* way.

When you take your partner for granted, you're coasting as a lover.

You sometimes work overtime at your job, right? —Why not work overtime on your relationship this week?!

*Don't coast! Relationships in **Neutral** end-up in **Reverse!***

Treat your anniversaries as "Personal Holidays."

Have a wedding cake made for your next anniversary!

Celebrate your anniversary every *month*.

Get a bottle of vintage wine from the year of your wedding.

Greet him at the door in your wedding gown!

Read your wedding vows to one another.

Why is world peace so hard to accomplish? Because it is essentially about love, and no one really understands love very well.

War is not about territory or resources or power. It's about *fear*. And fear is the lack of love.

The history of humankind is the story of our search for love.

*The quietly brave,
the creatively intimate,
the gently strong—they are
the lovers, the peace-makers,
the saviors of the world.*

Do you live your values?

Do you express your love?

Do you give of yourself?

Do you share yourself?

Do you listen?

Are you growing every day?

Are you considerate?

Are you trusting?

This is what romance is all about. Come to think of it, this is what *life* is all about!

Enjoy yourself
Express yourself
Reveal yourself
Share yourself
Know thyself
Love yourself
Develop yourself
Risk yourself
Be yourself
Give yourself

— The Lovers' Bedside Companion —

About the Author

Gregory J.P. Godek is a writer, lecturer and newlywed. He is the author of three bestselling books based on his 14 years of teaching Romance Seminars. Greg has appeared on the *Oprah Winfrey Show* conducting a "Mini-Romance Class"; and he has been featured on *The Donahue Show* discussing "Is Your Lover Among the Romantically Impaired?"

Greg speaks nationally and internationally, presenting keynote speeches and seminars on love and relationships. His first two books (*1001 Ways To Be Romantic* and *1001 More Ways To Be Romantic*) are *idea* books, presenting numbered listings of creative ideas, tips and resources. His third book (*Romance 101*) is a *lesson* book, presenting 64 lessons on topics such as "Spontaneity," "Communication," and "Intimacy." Greg now has one million books in print.

A companion to *this* book is being published simultaneously. Whereas *The Lovers' Bedside Companion* is an *inspirational* book, The *Portable Romantic* is a *practical* book, listing hundreds of new romantic ideas, secrets, schemes, rules, lessons and tips. Greg calls these two new books "Romantic Secret Weapons."

Romantic Things To Do Today

_____
_____
_____

Lessons to Review

_____
_____
_____

Romantic Plans for Next Week

_____
_____
_____

Personal Affirmations

_____
_____
_____

Romantic Plans for Next Month

_____
_____
_____

Romantic Shopping List

_____
_____
_____

Romantic Plans for Next Year

_____
_____
_____

Misc. Romantic Ideas

_____
_____
_____

Author's Note

Thank you for investing your time, your resources, your *self*, in enhancing your capacity to love. I believe that there is *nothing* you can do in your *entire life* that will pay-back more dividends than **learning to love.**

For those of you who are new to these books—*welcome!* Please join us on the Journey. I sometimes play the *guide*, but more often I'm a fellow traveller. Let's explore together.

For those of you who are old friends—*welcome back!* How've you been?

Here we go again!

Namaste,

~ G.J.P.G.

An Invitation

These books and seminars are part of the Grand Conversation, as Greg calls it. He sees his books as "The beginning of a *dialogue*, and not merely another long-winded monologue by some so-called 'expert'." We would like to hear from *you*.

You are invited to write to us with your romantic ideas and your romantic stories—whether sentimental, outrageous or creative. They may end up in the *LoveLetter* newsletter, or perhaps in a future book. We will credit you by name or protect your anonymity, as you wish. —Or just write to say *Hi!*

Romantic Ideas
Casablanca Press, Inc.
Post Office Box 226
Weymouth, Massachusetts
02188-0001

The "LoveLetter" Newsletter

- ❤ A free one-year subscription to the newsletter of romantic ideas—*The LoveLetter*—is now available for the asking!

- ❤ It's a $25 value, and it's full of creative, unusual and wonderful ideas, tips, gifts, gestures and resources.

- ❤ Sign-up yourself, your spouse, your boyfriend/girlfriend, your parents, your friends—anyone who needs a good swift kick-in-the-pants, or would simply appreciate receiving *lots* of great romantic ideas on a regular basis.

- ❤ And as long as you're writing, why don't you send-in your favorite creative ideas, great gift finds, special gestures. You'll be credited by name!

LoveLetter
Post Office Box 226
Weymouth, Massachusetts
02188-0001

To Order Books Directly

- ❤ *1001 Ways To Be Romantic*, 276 pages, softbound ($11.95)
- ❤ *1001 Ways To Be Romantic*, 276 pages, hardbound ($18.95)

- ☆ *1001 More Ways To Be Romantic*, 308 pages, softbound ($11.95)
- ☆ *1001 More Ways To Be Romantic*, 308 pages, hardbound ($18.95)

- ✦ *Romance 101*, 270 pages, softbound ($12.95)
- ✦ *Romance 101*, 270 pages, hardbound ($18.95)

- ☞ *The Lovers' Bedside Companion,* 160 pages, softbound ($6.95)
- ☞ *The Portable Romantic,* 160 pages, softbound ($6.95)

Call Toll-Free
800-444-2524

Extension 65

Major credit cards accepted.
Overnight delivery & regular delivery available: Different shipping charges apply.